Norman Rockwell

A CLASSIC TREASURY

February 13, 1960   *15¢*

EACH ACCORDING TO THE DICTATES OF · HIS OWN CONSCIENCE

NORMAN ROCKWELL

Norman Rockwell

A CLASSIC TREASURY

Robin Langley Sommer

BARNES
&NOBLE
BOOKS
NEW YORK

This edition published by
Barnes & Noble, Inc.,
by arrangement with Brompton Books Corporation.

Produced by Brompton Books Corporation
15 Sherwood Place
Greenwich, CT 06830

ISBN 1-56619-185-8

Printed in Spain
Reprinted 1995

Acknowledgments
The publisher and author would like to thank Bobby Moore, who
designed this book, and Sara Dunphy, who did the picture research.
Special thanks are due to the Norman Rockwell Family Trust for
permission to reproduce the plates and to the Curtis Archives for
valuable assistance in doing so. Thanks are also due the following
organizations for permission to reproduce other illustrations:
The Bettmann Archives: p. 11
The Springer/Betteman Archives: p. 17 (both)
UPI/Bettmann Newsphotos: pp. 7, 12 (top), 14 (both), 15, 19, 20

Page 1:
Triple Self-Portrait
Post cover, February 13, 1960

Page 2:
Freedom of Worship
poster, 1943, from the Series ''The
Four Freedoms.''

Right:
Stockbridge at Christmas
McCall's illustration, December 1967

CONTENTS

Norman Rockwell the Artist

Norman Rockwell's unique position in American painting and illustration results from an historical convergence of talent, timing, and sensitivity. Today, some 15 years after his death, he is still the nation's best-loved artist, perhaps the only artist known by name of millions of average people. Technique alone does not account for it, although Rockwell's powers of draftsmanship, lighting, composition, mood, character, and caricature were of the highest order. Hard work, good training, and meticulous research all played their parts. So did a sure instinct for the panorama of twentieth-century life in the United States, as he portrayed it for more than half a century. But above all was the deep affection Rockwell brought to his familiar subjects – an affection his audience returned in kind.

Rockwell's career began in 1912, at a time when illustration was moving rapidly into a place among the fine arts. The years between 1880 and 1920 saw revolutionary developments in printing technology. Mechanical photoengraving replaced the cumbersome process of hand engraving (woodcuts or lithographs) that had limited great nineteenth-century illustrators such as Howard Pyle and Frederic Remington. The halftone screen made it possible to reproduce photographs accurately for the first time, in black and white and, shortly thereafter, in color. Process color printing became faster and more affordable for the newspapers and magazines that were the nation's primary media of mass communication until halfway through the twentieth century, when television

challenged the printed word as nothing else had done. But television was only an idea when millions of middle-class Americans looked forward eagerly to the arrival of *The Saturday Evening Post, Collier's Weekly, Leslie's, Life* (originally a humor magazine), *Country Gentleman,* and *Literary Digest.* Popular juvenile magazines included *St. Nicholas, Youth's Companion, Harper's Young People*, and *Boys' Life*, the official magazine of the Boy Scouts of America. These publications and many others constituted a strong market for the work of young writers and artists, who came to the large cities in hopes of establishing themselves. By the 1920s many talented illustrators were heroes and heroines of popular culture, among them Maxfield Parrish, James Montgomery Flagg, Coles Phillips, Charles Dana Gibson of "Gibson Girl" fame, and the Leyendecker brothers, Joseph and Francis (Frank).

Book illustration, too, was both staple and showcase for gifted artists. Childrens' literature was especially important. Howard Pyle, a major influence on the Golden Age of Illustration, taught other artists as founder of the Brandywine School, which inspired N. C Wyeth, Violet Oakley, and, indirectly, Rockwell. Pyle was famous for his children's books, which were considered classics long before his death in 1911.

In addition to his graphic talent, and his appreciation for the power of pictures, Pyle was also a writer. A boy at the time of the Civil War, he began contributing stories, pictures, and cover designs to the nation's leading periodicals in 1876. He

Norman Rockwell in 1939, when he was 45.

Rockwell's 1935 painting *Dover Coach* is
typical of the Dickensian subject matter of
which he was always so fond.

admitted that, from his youth, he had preferred "book pictures" to "wall pictures." Both children and adults were captivated by his *Robin Hood, King Arthur and His Knights, The Champions of the Round Table*, and *The Wonder Clock*, and most of his books are still in print at this writing. Pyle was reaching his artistic maturity at the age of 31 when Norman Rockwell was born, on February 3, 1894.

Unlike most young people who hoped to make their mark as artists, Norman Rockwell did not have to go to the big city: he was a New Yorker born and bred. The fact that he came from a literary and artistic family was an additional advantage. His father, Jarvis Waring Rockwell, manager of the New York office of George Woods, Sons, and Company, a textile firm, read Dickens to his sons, Norman and Jarvis, and by an early age Norman was drawing the characters from *The Pickwick Papers* and other classics as he listened to the stories. Dickensian themes would, in fact, appear often in his future work, especially in his Christmas covers for the *Post*. His mother, Nancy Hill Rockwell, was the daughter of Thomas Hill, an English painter who had emigrated to the United States in the 1860s. She traced her mother's family back to Sir Norman Percevel, and her oldest son was the beneficiary of both these ancestral names. However, "Percevel" was conspicuous by its absence from his signature. ("Do you wonder I dropped it?" he would ask a biographer.)

While his family lived in New York City, until he was nine years old, Rockwell sang with the choir at St. Luke's Episcopal Church and later at the Cathedral of St. John the Divine. He was a slender child, nearsighted and pigeon-toed,

which excluded him from many sports, but that did not greatly affect his popularity, for his talent for drawing entertained his contemporaries. He looked forward to summers spent in the country, in rural New Jersey and upstate New York.

In 1903 his family moved to Mamaroneck, in nearby Westchester County, New York. His interest in art continued to grow, and by the age of 14 he had already decided to make it his career. He began taking lessons at New York's Chase School of Fine and Applied Art, and shortly thereafter he dropped out of high school to become a full-time student at the National Academy School.

Classical training at the National Academy School proved tedious. The students spent long hours making charcoal studies of Greek and Roman sculptures cast in plaster – copies of copies. They studied anatomy, proportion, and rendering long before they saw their first live model, and still lifes were a prominent part of the curriculum. Within a year Rockwell transferred to the more progressive Art Students League, one of whose founders was his lifelong hero, Howard Pyle. In this far more stimulating environment, where illustration was taken seriously and taught professionally, he came into his own. His talent flourished under the guidance of such mentors as Thomas Fogarty and George Bridgman, the latter an inspired teacher of artist's anatomy, and he was encouraged to seek outside assignments.

In fact, Rockwell had received his first commission at the age of 16, when he designed four Christmas cards for Mrs. Arnold Constable, of the affluent department-store family. A year later he illustrated his first children's book: C. H. Claudy's

Tell-Me-Why Stories About Mother Nature. By the time he and his family moved back to New York City in 1912 he was receiving enough commissions to become a full-time illustrator, and he was able to rent his first studio in an attic on the Upper West Side.

Rockwell began contributing to *Boys' Life* in 1912, when he was hired to illustrate one of the Boy Scout handbooks. At the age of 19 he became art director of the magazine. Some of his earliest published work appeared in the *Boy Scouts Hike Book* and the *Boys Camp Book*, and his loyal relationship with the Boy Scouts of America would continue for the rest of his life. At the same time, he was free to contribute to other youth-oriented magazines such as *St Nicholas* and *Youth's Companion*. During this period he drew and painted mainly what he knew best – boys – and this theme would carry over to his earliest advertising work, such as his 1919 ads for Fisk Bicycle Tires. Advertising paid better than the magazines, and Rockwell received many such commissions during his career, but he always preferred the relatively greater freedom of interior and cover illustrations. To be sure, publishers imposed many exacting requirements as well, but the advertising agencies exercised far more control over style and content, and the latter was almost always restricted to products or scenes in which people were using them.

In 1915 the Rockwell family moved back to Westchester County, this time to the town of New Rochelle. Rockwell

A young Rockwell and even younger model.

accompanied them, renting a studio for his work and mixing with many of the famous illustrators who lived in the New York suburb at the time. Charles Dana Gibson, also an Art Students League alumnus; the Leyendecker brothers; and Howard Chandler Christy, who went on to paint *The Signing of the Constitution*, which hangs in the Capitol rotunda in Washington, D.C., were only some of the artists who then graced New Rochelle's lively social scene. In 1916 Rockwell secured his professional place in this high-powered group when his first cover appeared on the nation's most widely-read magazine, *The Saturday Evening Post.* Published on May 20, 1916, it depicted a well-dressed boy, complete with bowler hat, being jeered at by his baseball-playing friends as he pushed a baby carriage. Not only did the *Post's* art director, Walter Dower, accept this painting on Rockwell's first visit, he bought a second painting of a children's backyard circus and asked Rockwell to complete a sketch of an elderly man playing baseball with children. These were among the themes most in demand by American magazines of the day, and Norman Rockwell was, by both taste and training, clearly the man to paint them.

Rockwell soon followed this professional milestone with a personal one – his marriage to Irene O'Connor, a schoolteacher from Potsdam, New York. Just as the young Rockwells were taking their rightful place in the commercial art world, however, the United States entered the Great War that had been raging in Europe since 1914. Rockwell joined the Navy in the summer of 1918 and was sent to the Charleston, South Carolina, navy yard for the duration. His efforts to serve overseas were frustrated, and he had little to do save spending a few days a week working for the service magazine *Afloat and Ashore.* This left ample time for his regular clients, including not only the *Post* but eight or nine other major magazines and such advertisers as Perfection oil heaters, Overland automobiles, Jell-O, and Orange Crush.

When he returned to New Rochelle, Rockwell was not only famous but rich enough eventually to build a $23,000 studio in the then-popular Early American style. He was invited to help choose Miss America; traveled to Europe, South America, and North Africa; drank bootleg whisky during Prohibition; and studied modern art in 1923, when he attended classes at Calorossi's art school during a trip to Paris. However, the *Post's* redoubtable editor, George Lorimer, who recognized Rockwell's genius for the evocation of everyday life, encouraged him to continue and perfect what he did best. Their association, marked by mutual warmth and confidence, would continue until Lorimer's retirement in 1936, and Rockwell's relationship with the *Post* would endure until 1963.

From the outset, Rockwell had a deep affinity for the themes that established him in the hearts of his audience: childhood and family life, young love, leavetakings and homecomings, youth and age, and holiday celebrations. He painted a Christmas cover for the *Post* every year from 1919 until 1943, and his work was in great demand for Christmas calendars as well. Even when he painted winter scenes with no reference to Christmas, they were often identified with his holiday paintings. During the 1920s his Christmas paintings included five *Post* covers featuring Santa Claus and five period covers with a Dickensian theme. Thanksgiving, that uniquely American holiday, was a close second in popularity. It was treated humorously in a 1921 cover for *Life*, entitled *A Pilgrim's Progress*, in which a boy in Puritan garb carrying a large turkey flees a volley of Indian arrows. The popular ''Cousin Reginald'' series for *Country Gentleman* included a 1917 holiday cover in which the turkey is chasing the citified Cousin Reginald, who has come out to dispatch it for the family dinner — his country cousins are laughing in the background. That year's Christmas cover, *Cousin Reginald Under the Mistletoe*, featured a very pretty girl — probably the all-time favorite cover subject ever since Victorian times.

Rockwell's work was usually strongly narrative, but in some of his early work he carried this tendency to the extreme of illustrating his subjects' thoughts by means of mental images hovering above the principal figure, painted in a different tonal scale to keep the two distinct. An example is the *Post* Christmas cover for 1920, in which Santa Claus ponders his budget against a background of children's faces enclosed by a large circle below the title. (The following year Rockwell's illustration would break the title lettering for the first time.) A 1923 cover of a boy reading a book about knighthood introduced a series of affecting ''mental image'' covers, including one of a clerk daydreaming about adventures on the high seas and a one-legged pirate dreaming of the home he had left as a boy.

Since animals are inseparable from the home-and-family scene, an engaging menagerie appears in Rockwell's work —

everything from the predictable puppies and kittens to *The Lion and His Keeper* (*Post*, January 9, 1954), in which the recumbent lion wistfully eyes the keeper's sandwich through the bars. An unbudgable bulldog in an alleyway stops a truck in *Traffic Conditions* (1949), and no veterinarian's office is complete without its framed copy of *Waiting for the Vet*, which appeared on the *Post's* cover on March 29, 1952. In two consecutive *Country Gentleman* covers of 1921 – *Bully Before* and *Bully After* – the victor's dog chases the bully's dog from the scene when the astonished young human bully is knocked down by his intended victim.

Since Rockwell painted from live models rather than photographs until the mid-1930s, his studio must sometimes have been reminiscent of Old McDonald's farm when he was working on animal scenes. His autobiography contains a wild account of his struggle to pose a chicken: "You pick up the chicken and rock him back and forth a few times. When you set him down he will stand just as you've placed him for four or five minutes. Of course, you have to run behind the easel pretty quickly to do much painting before the chicken moves. But it's better than trying to paint him while he's dashing about the studio . . . It's very strenuous painting a chicken."

Throughout the 1920s Rockwell grew in both proficiency and popularity. At the end of the decade his divorce from Irene Rockwell was followed by a return to New York City, where he lived for some time at the Hotel des Artistes. He was now entering upon a new phase of his career, a period of extremely rapid development that would, by the end of the decade of the 1930s, produce the mature style for which he is best remembered and most admired.

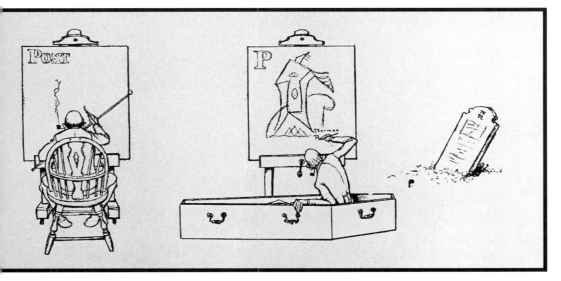

Opposite:
Rockwell illustrations for the 1913 *Boy Scouts Hike Book.*

Above left and right:
Rockwell demonstrates poses to some of his amateur sitters.

Left:
In a serial cartoon, *Norman Rockwell From the Cradle to the Grave* (1946), the artist predicts (wrongly) that he will be doing *Post* covers forever.

On an extended trip to California in 1930 Rockwell met and married Mary Barstow, a young California schoolteacher. Their first child, Jarvis (called Jerry) was born in 1932 in New Rochelle, where the Rockwells had been living since their marriage. That year also saw a lengthy trip to Paris, which confirmed Rockwell's belief that his artistic strength was in painting what he knew best in his own style, which grew increasingly naturalistic. By this time he was doing covers almost exclusively for the *Post* and accepting more commissions for interior illustration. Then in 1935 Heritage Press approached him with a request for a series of 16 paintings for a deluxe edition of the Twain classics *The Adventures of Tom Sawyer* and *Huckleberry Finn*: it was a challenge he welcomed.

With his usual diligence, Rockwell researched the period in depth, even traveling to Hannibal, Missouri, to see the setting of Twain's stories and interview local people. There he bought clothing and other props that would, along with the many sketches he had made, help him create the final paintings of Tom, Huck, and their world along the Mississippi. The illustrations were among the best he had ever done, and this commission was followed by an equally successful foray into children's literature for the *Woman's Home Companion*. Katharine Anthony had written a series on Louisa May Alcott, "Most Beloved American Writer," for which Rockwell was invited to do the illustrations. He did the same kind of research on Alcott in Concord, Massachusetts, that he had done in Hannibal, and the series was published to general acclaim between December 1937 and March 1938.

That year the Rockwells took another trip to Europe with all three of their children, now including Tommy, born in 1933, and Peter, two years old. Rockwell's *Post* covers from this

Above:
Rockwell and his bride, Mary Rhodes Barstow, at their wedding in 1930.

period reflect the shift in his point of view on family life, from observer to participant. Humorous *Post* paintings of this period include *Tantrum* (October 24, 1936) and *Spirit of Education* (April 21, 1934), in which an extremely reluctant little boy is decked out for the school pageant in toga, sandals, and laurel wreath. His expression is among the most memorable in all Rockwell's work.

The 1934 painting *Land of Enchantment* captures the depth of Rockwell's feeling for children's literature, and shows as well, the influence of such artists as John Tenniel, who illustrated *Alice's Adventures in Wonderland*, and George Cruikshank, perhaps best remembered for his drawings for Dickens's *Oliver Twist*. But it was solely Rockwell's interpretation of Dickens that produced the memorable *Tiny Tim and Bob Cratchit*, Rockwell's 1934 Christmas cove for the *Post*.

In 1939 Rockwell and his wife began to look for a place in the country, and in the end they found just the kind of "home town" most people had assumed he came from: Arlington, Vermont, north of Bennington. The Rockwells were to spend 14 years there, very much at home with the sturdy, independent spirit of the region and the natural beauty of the Vermont countryside. In time, other artists migrated to Arlington, among them Mead Schaeffer, Jack Atherton, and George Hughes, all of whom Rockwell knew from the *Post*. By this time, George Lorimer had resigned as editor, to be succeeded by Wesley Stout. During the 1930s, Rockwell had painted 67 covers for the *Post*, and as the decade moved to a close, new patterns began to appear in his work. There was a greater sense of tranquility, a more subtle blending of humor and pathos. These tendencies would deepen during the World War II years.

In 1940 Rockwell traveled to Washington to present his poster for a children's war relief drive to President Franklin D. Roosevelt. That same year he was honored by the Art Directors

Above:
A sketch of the Pont Neuf in Paris made by Rockwell in 1932.

Opposite bottom:
"Fontainebleau," 1932.

Left:
A watercolor of the Pont Neuf, also dating from the 1932 trip to Paris.

Above:
Rockwell in Vermont in 1950.

Club for the best advertising poster of the year. Many other artists were by now working in his manner, but none so successfully. The national unity engendered by the war, the sense of shared values at grave risk, the effort on the home front – all found their expression in Rockwell's work. His creation of Willie Gillis, the young G.I. whom he followed from basic training to postwar college, was inspired. His model was Robert Buck, an Arlington neighbor, and after Buck's enlistment in 1943, Rockwell continued the series by painting photographs of Willie Gillis into home-front scenes like *The Fighting Gillises*. In this 1944 *Post* cover Willie's photograph takes its place on the mantel with family portraits of "fighting Gillises" from the American Revolution to World War I. Below them is a set of books, including *Gillis at Gettysburg, Gillis and Lincoln,* and *Victory with Gillis*. For years afterward, readers were writing to find out where they could get these imaginary works.

In 1942 Rockwell began a series of four paintings of ordinary Americans in scenes that portrayed the ideals for which the nation had gone to war. Called *The Four Freedoms*, the sequence included *Freedom of Worship, Freedom of Speech, Freedom from Fear* and *Freedom from Want*. These were not designed primarily as illustrations, but as original works, and as such they were seen by more than a million people on a 16-city tour on behalf of war bonds: the tour raised more than $130 million. The *Post* had just before that published the pictures as inside illustrations in 1943, and its millions of readers had reacted just as strongly. Government agencies that had turned down the sequence when Rockwell offered it to them as a public service soon realized their error. *The Four Freedoms* had

struck a chord that reverberated across the country.

Rockwell's war effort continued, undeterred by the 1943 studio fire that destroyed many irreplaceable paintings and his entire collection of antique costumes and properties, correspondence, books, and many sketches. Vermont neighbors helped him to rebuild in nearby West Arlington and contributed heirloom clothing to replace his lost collection. Although Rockwell characteristically made light of the experience in a series of sketches for the *Post*, it was a heavy blow, alleviated only by the prompt help and kindness it occasioned.

Memorable *Post* covers of the war years included *Rosie the Riveter*, the November 1943 Thanksgiving picture of a war refugee wearing a soldier's jacket and saying grace over a mess kit, and seven different portrayals of homecoming servicemen and their families. One of these was the much-loved 1945 painting *Home for Thanksgiving*, in which a G.I. is contentedly at work peeling potatoes with his mother at home instead of on K.P. The setting for another such cover, *Homecoming G.I.,* is a gritty mill-town tenement rather than an idyllic country village. Increasingly, Rockwell was painting contemporary life as he saw it, unfiltered by nostalgia.

After the war Rockwell began a long series of calendars depicting the four seasons for Brown & Bigelow, many of them featuring boys playing team sports. Hallmark commissioned the first of its Christmas cards from him, and artists' trade magazines such as *Art News* and *Art Digest* celebrated his work. In 1948 he began his association with the Famous Artists School in Westport, Connecticut, then newly established as a correspondence course for aspiring writers and illustrators. The

Opposite top:
Rockwell presents President Roosevelt with the original painting of a 1940 poster.

Left:
The Art Directors Club gives Rockwell the award for best advertising poster in 1940.

The all-time favorite Rockwell *Post* cover,
according to a reader survey, was his 1951
painting *Saying Grace*.

school was highly regarded and flourished into the 1970s, when the decline of the great illustrated magazines eventually resulted in its demise due to the shrinking market for illustration.

The 1950s were transitional years for America, filled with social and intellectual changes produced by the war, the ensuing Cold War, and the impact of new technologies. Television began to have its far-reaching effect upon mass communication. The country was becoming more urban in fact and more cosmopolitan in spirit. And there was a new ambivalence toward traditional values, although the full effect of this would not be felt until the following decade. Rockwell too, was beginning to be troubled – both by growing dissatisfaction with his work and by concern about his wife's increasingly severe depression. The couple traveled to Stockbridge, Massachusetts, in the Berkshires, where Mary Rockwell was successfully treated at the Austin-Riggs Center, and in 1953 the Rockwells moved to Stockbridge permanently. They soon became highly valued members of the community, which included other creative people associated with the Berkshire Playhouse and the music center at Tanglewood. Rockwell rented a studio over a row of shops on the town's picturesque Main Street, where he sometimes found a model among the residents who passed by. In 1957 he bought a Federal-style house in Stockbridge and relocated his studio to the converted carriage house behind it. His spirits improved, and he did some of his best-known covers for the *Post* during this decade, including *Breaking Home Ties, The Marriage License, After the Prom,* and *The Runaway.* Children and adolescents figured in more than half of the 41 covers Rockwell did for the *Post* during the 1950s, including the famous *Saying Grace,* a

painting that the magazine's readers would later vote their favorite of all his works.

At the same time, Rockwell carried out many advertising commissions and began a 12-year series for the Massachusetts Mutual Life Insurance Company. It featured the everyday experiences of a typical American family, from bathing the dog to bringing home a new baby, in pencil drawings that were executed in a straightforward realistic style of great immediacy. Although he had now been working partly from photographs for many years, the camera lens never replaced live models, many of them drawn from his wide circle of friends. A Rockwell sitting was a creative endeavor in itself, with the artist also dressing up to act out the poses and scenes he wanted.

Rockwell's interiors had become more detailed over the years. *Shuffleton's Barber Shop* (1950) is an impressive example – a mood piece that focuses on a group of amateur musicians seen through the window of a small barber shop that has closed for the day. The strong sense of community, the absolute fidelity to detail, and the almost magical lighting contribute to the power of this evocation of a time that was rapidly passing away.

The artist poses with the original of his 1961 *Post* cover *The Golden Rule.*

In 1952 Rockwell began to paint his portraits of Republican and Democratic presidential candidates, beginning with former general Dwight D. Eisenhower. Other celebrities appeared on the *Post's* cover later in the decade, including comedians Bob Hope and Jack Benny. Allusions to the inevitable passing of time also began to appear somewhat more frequently in his work during this period. Thus the Four Seasons calendar for 1956, *Two Old Friends*, adverted to the famous 1921 cover *No Swimming*, in which three half-dressed boys and a dog are running away from an irate pursuer who has surprised them at a swimming hole. In the 1956 version, it is two elderly men and a dog who are fleeing the scene.

In 1959 Mary Rockwell died suddenly of a heart attack. Rockwell's grief was compounded by professional concerns, including the declining circulation of the magazines that he worked for and mounting criticism from those who charged that his work was no longer socially or politically relevant. In a 1960 article for *Atlantic Monthly*, Wright Morris even went so far as to accuse Rockwell of ''destroying the taste of American people'' by neglecting trends in modern art. As the national consensus on moral and political issues continued to erode, many magazines, including the *Post*, tried desperately to revise their content, but with little success: the days when mass-circulation magazines could depend on single, homogeneous readerships seemed to be slipping away.

In 1961 Rockwell married Molly Punderson, a retired teacher from Milton Academy, who had grown up in Stockbridge. His ties to the community remained strong and helped him to weather the blow he suffered in 1963, when *The Saturday Evening Post* ended its 47-year relationship with him. New editorial policies held that Rockwell's images and ideas were now out of date. His last *Post* cover appeared on

Rockwell stands beside a group of the celebrated ''multiple portraits'' that he executed during the 1960s.

In 1961 Rockwell married Molly
Punderson, a former teacher.

December 14, 1963: a portrait of President John F. Kennedy, who had been assassinated the month before. It was the 420th cover he had done for the *Post*. But the *Post's* decision to try to do without Rockwell proved at best irrelevant; its circulation continued to plunge, and the magazine went under shortly thereafter. Four years later, it was revived under new management as a magazine devoted to nostalgia. It still held the rights to many of Rockwell's earlier paintings, and these were frequently used inside the new magazine.

The positive side of Rockwell's break with the *Post* was that he, now almost 70 years old, was free to accept commissions from other magazines, and offers flowed into the Stockbridge studio. *McCall's* commissioned several large landscapes of Stockbridge, including the well-known panoramic view of Main Street at Christmastime. *Look* invited him to paint major news events, including school desegregation in the South, which resulted in the memorable picture entitled *The Problem We All Live With*. A small black girl in white is being escorted past a wall splattered with tomatoes and racist graffiti: the U.S. marshals who accompany her are seen only partially, as faceless figures in grey. Rockwell would take up the theme of integration again in the thoughtful painting *New Kids in the Neighborhood*.

In 1964 Rockwell undertook a series of multiple portraits of famous political leaders for *Look*. These included Lyndon Johnson, Ronald Reagan, Richard Nixon, and Robert F. Kennedy. He made a similarly distinguished portrait of the philosopher Bertrand Russell for Ramparts. The National Aeronautics and Space Administration (NASA) invited him to join a group of artists chosen to depict the conquest of space, and he roamed freely through the restricted areas of Cape Canaveral and the Space Center at Houston, making sketches of the program in action. These were published with those of the other artists involved in the book *Eyewitness to Space*. Later, *Look* asked him to do a series of illustrations on space exploration, including *Man's First Step on the Moon*. The artist who had once sketched doughboys during World War I was, more than 40 years later, still recording momentous events in American history.

In 1960 *The Saturday Evening Post* had published Rockwell's memoirs as "The Adventures of an Illustrator." (This lively autobiography, as told to Tommy Rockwell, was published later in book form.) In 1968 a retrospective exhibition of Rockwell's work was held at New York City's Dannenberg Gallery. It awakened a new appreciation for his paintings, most of which had never been seen except in reproduction. But in the closing years of Rockwell's life, his overriding themes, home and family, were still under attack from many sources. As a lifelong professional, he had always tried to shift his focus with the times and to meet the new needs of his clientele — and his public. The innocent world of his early work had given way to a wider view toward the mid-century, as the nation became increasingly urbanized. The impact of World War II has been indelibly imprinted on his canvases. Yet when the times changed again, he was attacked not for what he was doing currently but for what he had done in the past.

It seems appropriate that Rockwell's last cover was the one for *American Artist* in the Bicentennial year of 1976. He painted himself placing a banner on the Liberty Bell that reads "Happy Birthday." That same year he was honored by the Norman Rockwell Parade in Stockbridge — the longest in the town's history. A year later he received the President's Medal of Freedom, one of many awards that marked his last years. At last, on November 8, 1978, he died at his home in Stockbridge at the age of 84.

Critical and popular reappraisals of Norman Rockwell as artist and illustrator are still ongoing 15 years after his death. There was never any doubt about his technical brilliance, but recently there has been renewed appreciation for the storytelling dimension of his work, the authenticity he brought to it, and his deep affection for the people and places he drew and painted. His feeling for the beauty and importance of everyday life was of a rare order, and his ability to make others feel it as well was surely not far removed from genius. This gift for perceiving what E.B. White called the glory of everything is Norman Rockwell's most enduring legacy.

In 1976, two years before Rockwell's death, his home town, Stockbridge, Mass., honored him with a parade. It lasted for two hours.

The Plates

Above:
Outside the Principal's Office
Post cover, 1953.

Right:
Rosie the Riveter
Post cover, 1943.

THE SATURDAY EVENING POST

An Illustrated Weekly
Founded A.... 28 by Benj. Franklin

MAY 20, 1916

5c. THE COPY

Norman
Rockwell

THE EMPIRE BUILDERS—By Mary Roberts Rinehart

THE SATURDAY EVENING POST

Volume 202, Number 38

March 22, 1930

5c. The Copy
10c. in Canada

Owen Wister—Gilbert Seldes—Eleanor Mercein—Wallace Nutting
Roy Chapman Andrews—Thomas Beer—Lucian Cary—Ban Johnson

Left:
Boy with Carriage
Post cover, 1916.

Above:
Card Tricks
Post cover, 1930.

Left:
Volunteer Firemen
Post cover, 1931.

Above:
First Day in School
Post cover, 1935.

THE SATURDAY EVENING POST

Fou[nded] [by Benjamin Frank]lin

Volume 198, Number 52

JUNE 26, 1926

5c. the Copy

Earl Derr Biggers — Austin Parker — ... k Ward O'Malley — Isaac F. Marcosson
Edwin Balmer and William Mac Har ...wson ...phen Leacock — Henry Milner Rideout

Left:
The Scholar
Post cover, 1926.

Above:
Family Home from Vacation
Post cover, 1930.

The New Tavern Sign
Post illustration, 1936.

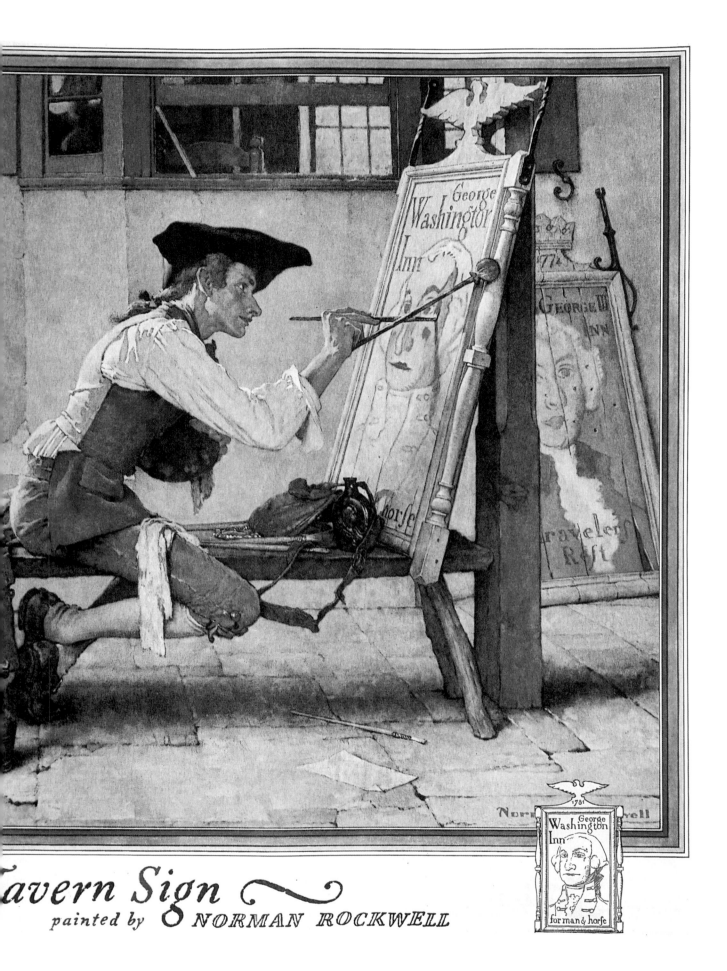

Tavern Sign
painted by *NORMAN ROCKWELL*

Above:
Checkup
Post cover, 1957.

Right:
Diary
Post cover, 1942.

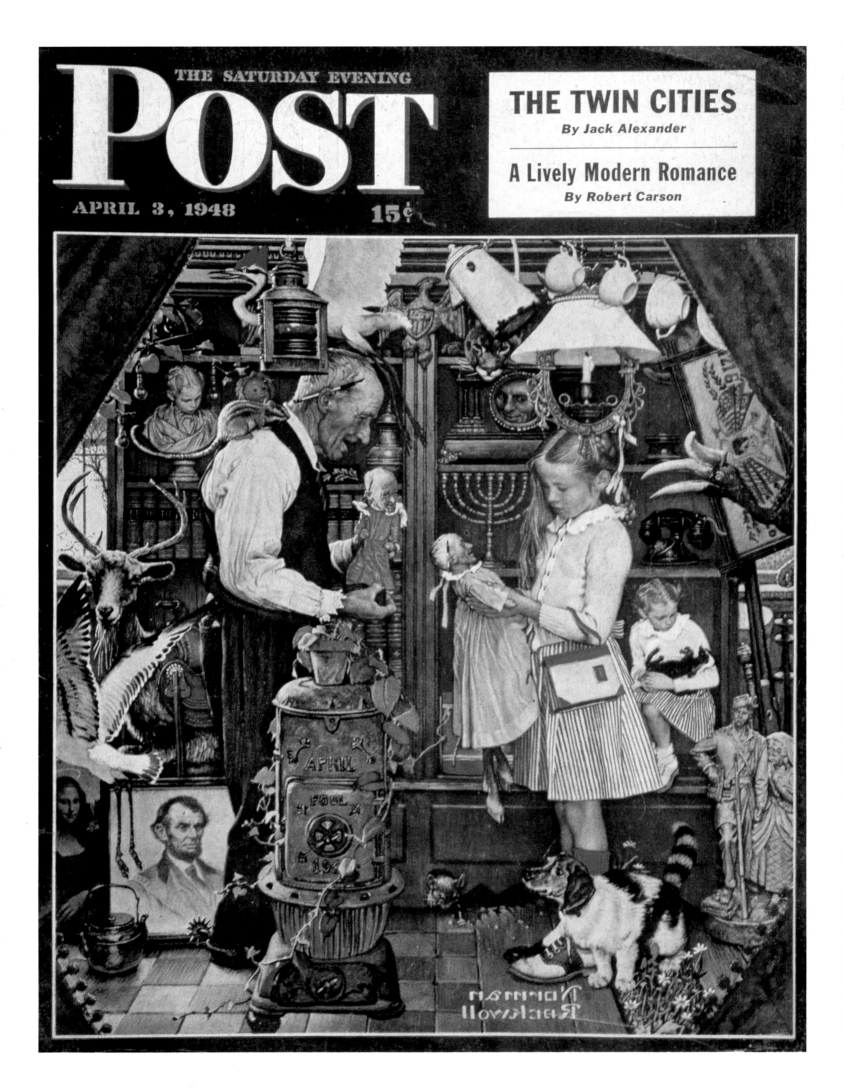

Left:
April Fool 1948
Post cover, 1948.

Above:
Willie Gillis at the USO
Post cover, 1942.

THE SATURDAY EVENING

POST

NOVEMBER 18, 1950   15¢

Above:
The Trumpeter
Post cover, 1950.

Right:
Clock Repairman
Post cover, 1945.

THE SATURDAY EVENING

POST

NOVEMBER 3, 1945   10¢

CHICAGO
By
GEORGE SESSIONS PERRY

—

Beginning a new
ALBRAND SERIAL

100th Year of Baseball
Post cover, 1939.

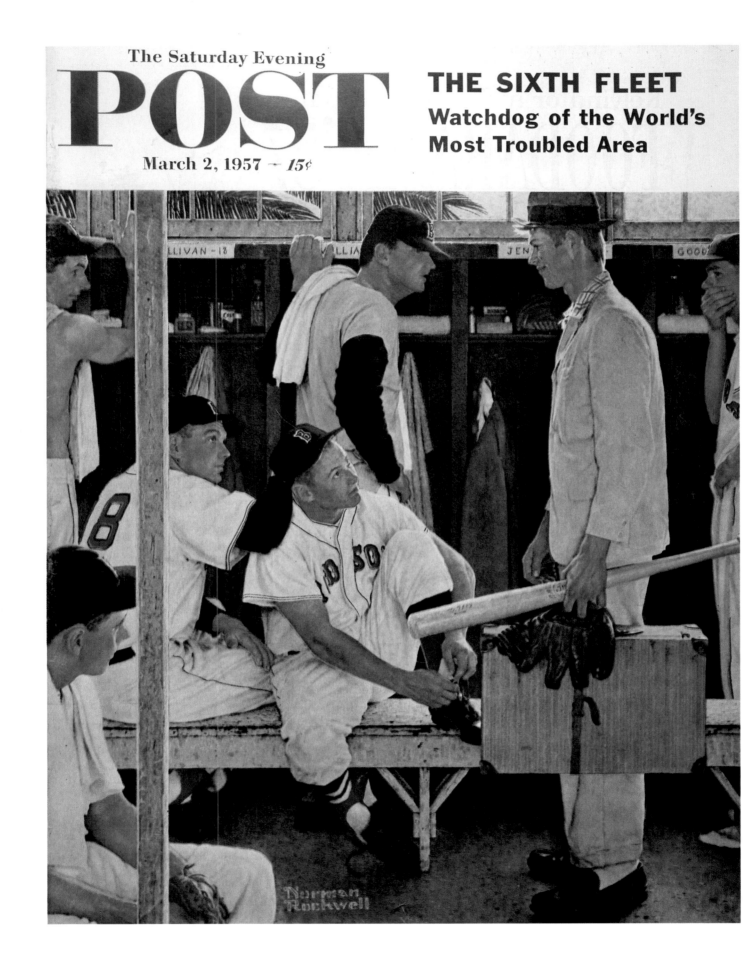

THE SIXTH FLEET

Watchdog of the World's
Most Troubled Area

The Locker Room
Post cover, 1957.

The Land of Enchantment
Post illustration, 1934.

Above:
Girl at the Mirror
Post cover, 1954.

Right:
The Bodybuilder
Post cover, 1922.

THE SATURDAY EVENING POST

Founded A.D. 1728 by Benjamin Franklin

5c.
10c. in Canada

APRIL 29, 1922

Norman Rockwell

IT'S EASY

BE A MAN

LESSON IX

CHAMP

Vol. 194, No. 44. Published weekly at Philadelphia. Entered as second-class matter,
November 18, 1879, at the Post Office at Philadelphia, under the Act of March 3, 1879.

In This Number
GEORGE PATTULLO — DANA BURNET — MARGUERITE CURTIS
RICHARD CONNELL — EVERETT RHODES CASTLE — JULIAN STREET

The Gossips
Post cover, 1948.

The Jury Holdout
Post cover, 1959.

45

THE SATURDAY EVENING

POST

SEPTEMBER 4, 1948   15¢

**IN DEFENSE OF THE
RUSSIAN PEOPLE**

By Alexander Barmine
FORMER SOVIET GENERAL

Norman Rockwell

The Saturday Evening

POST

February 16, 1952 — 15¢

I Was the Witness

WHITTAKER CHAMBERS'
OWN STORY OF THE TRIAL
OF ALGER HISS

VISITOR HOME
5 4   5 3

Left:
The Dugout
Post cover, 1948.

Above:
Losing the Game
Post cover, 1952.

48

Left:
The Diving Board
Post cover, 1947.

Above:
Game Called Because of Rain
Post cover, 1949.

THE SATURDAY EVENING POST

Volume 203, Number 19

NOV. 8,
1930

For . . . . in

10c. in Canada

5 cts.

Clarence Budington Kelland—Don Marquis—Boyden Sparkes—Travis Mason
John P. Marquand—Walter S. Gifford—Guy Gilpatric—Margaret C. Banning

Left:
The Milkmaid
Post cover, 1931.

Above:
The Yarn Spinner
Post cover, 1930.

Ice Cream Carrier
Post cover, 1940.

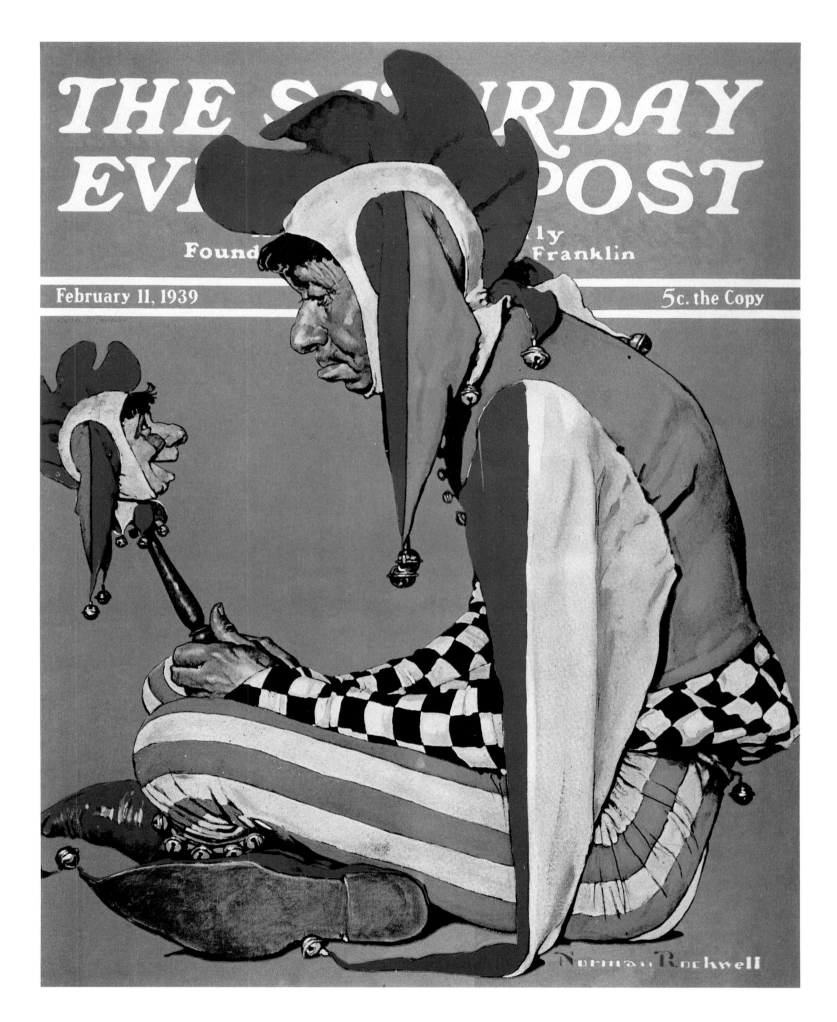

The Jesters
Post cover, 1939.

THE SATURDAY EVENING

POST

JULY 9, 1949   15¢

NORFOLK
By Richard Tregaskis
They're Cleaning Up Pennsylvania's
Foulest River—at Last

Left:
Lion and his Keeper
Post cover. 1954.

Above:
Traffic Conditions
Post cover, 1949.

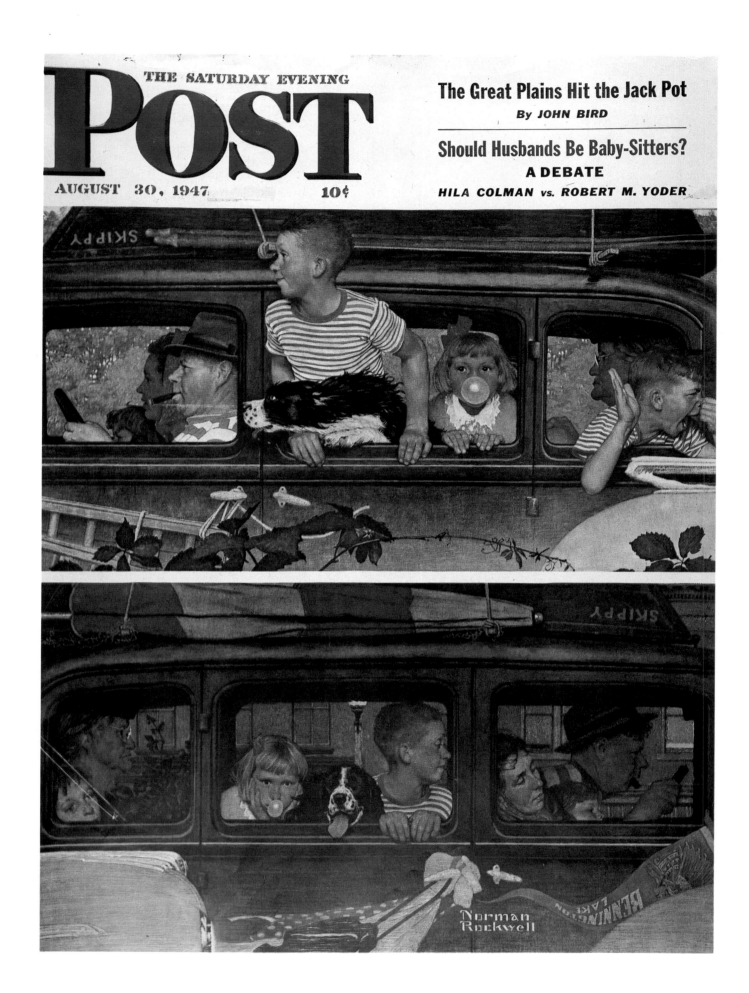

Above:
The Outing
Post cover, 1947.

Right:
Before the Date
Post cover, 1949.

THE SATURDAY EVENING

POST

SEPTEMBER 24, 1949   15¢

**WHAT'S BECOME OF
THE INFANTRY?**
By Beverly Smith

THAT MAN, Jr.
By Wesley Price

The Saturday Evening
POST
August 21, 1954 – 15¢

One Family's Ordeal:
OUR DAUGHTER HAD POLIO

**The Republicans Muffed
the Ball in Dixie**
By HODDING CARTER

Page 60:
Home Plate
Post cover, 1954.

Page 61:
No Looking
Post cover, 1929.

Left:
No Swimming
Post cover, 1921.

Above:
The Swimming Hole
Post cover, 1945.

New Kids in the Neighborhood
Look illustration, 1967.

Cousin Reginald Plays Pirate
Country Gentleman cover, 1917.

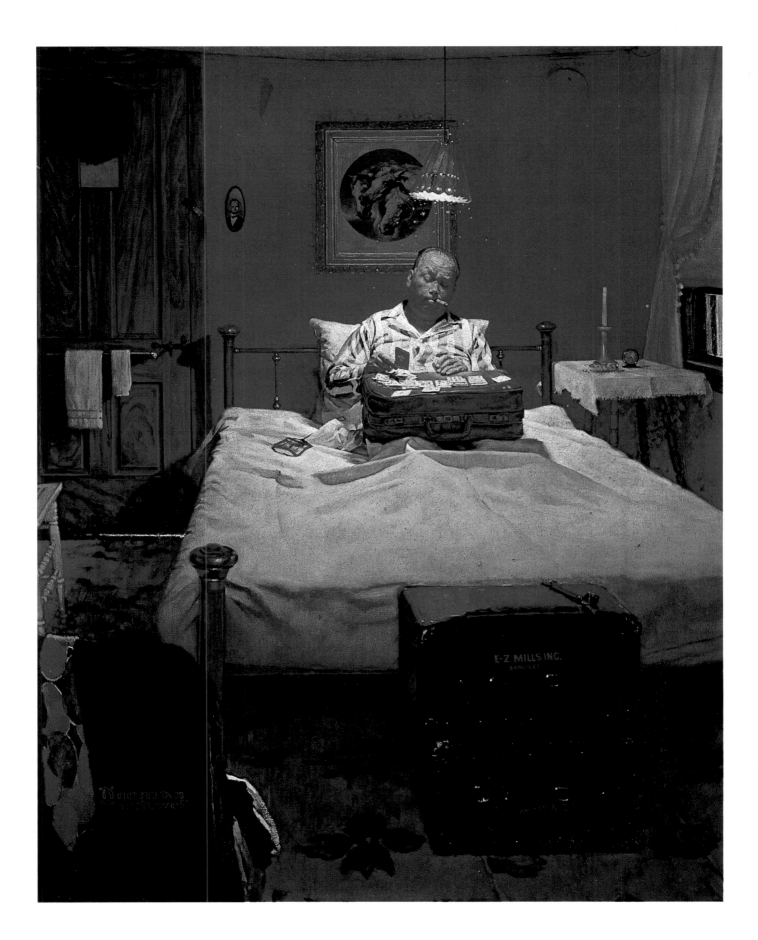

Solitaire
Post cover, 1950.

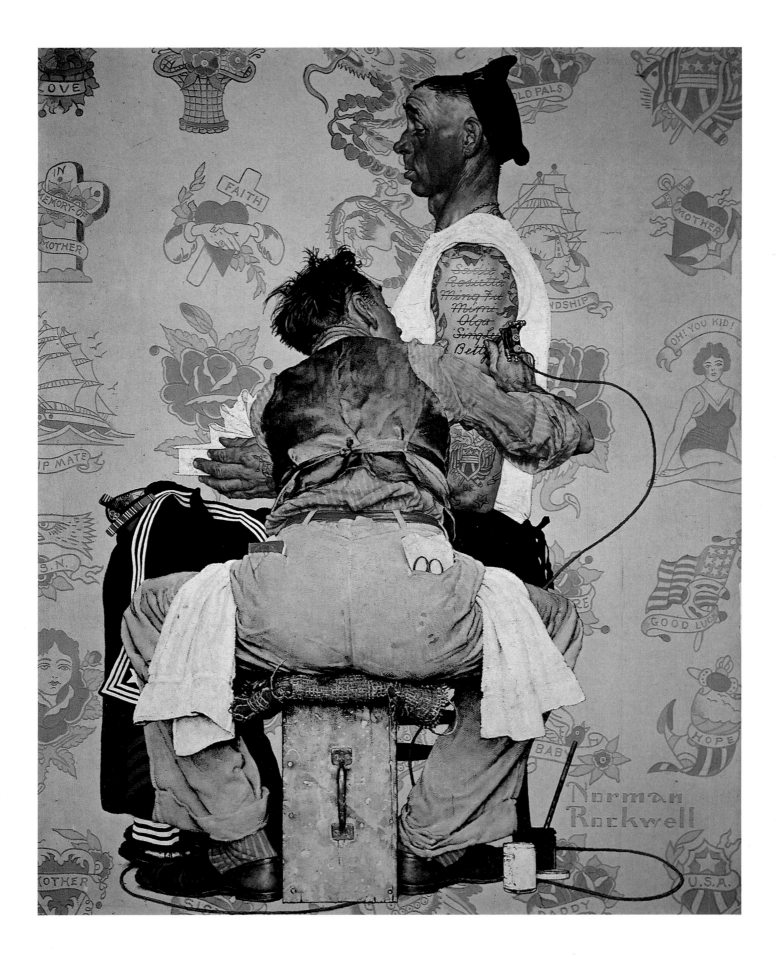

The Tattooist
Post cover, 1944.

Doctor and Doll
Post cover, 1929.

The Prom Dress
Post cover, 1949.

After the Prom
Post cover, 1957.

The Saturday Evening

POST

May 16, 1959 – *15¢*

Our Gamble With Destiny
By STEWART ALSOP

WARNING TO YOUNG MEN By Eric Sevareid

Above:
Easter Morning
Post cover, 1959.

Right:
The Spirit of Education
Post cover, 1934.

rockwell

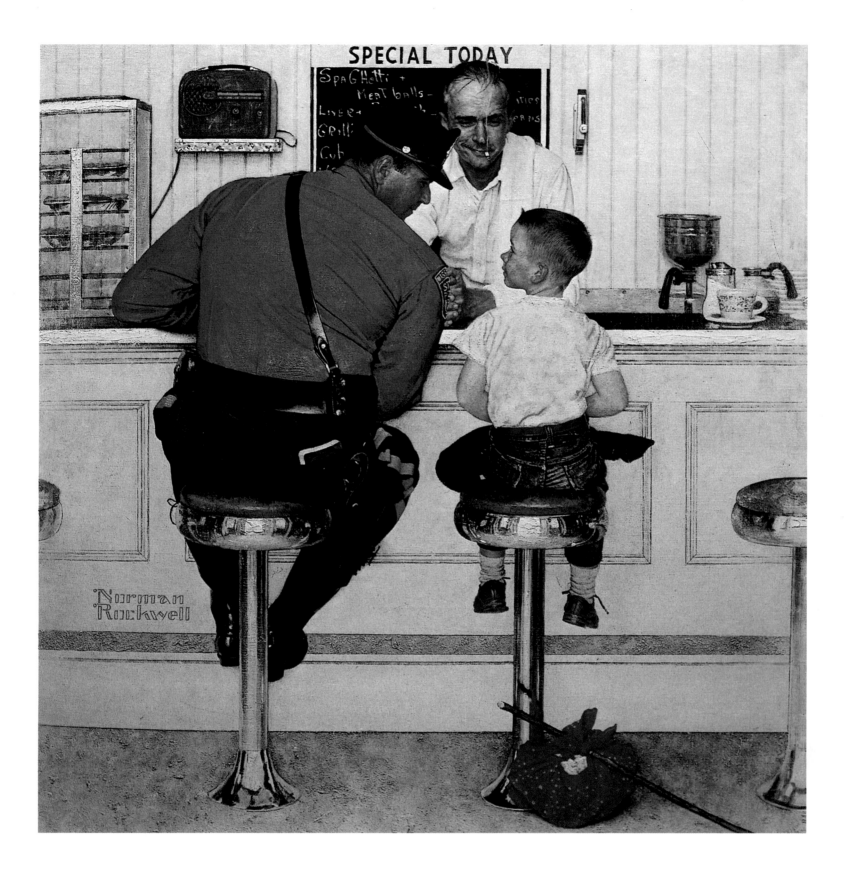

Pages 74-75:
The Problem We All Live With
Look illlustration, 1964

Above:
The Runaway
Post cover, 1958.

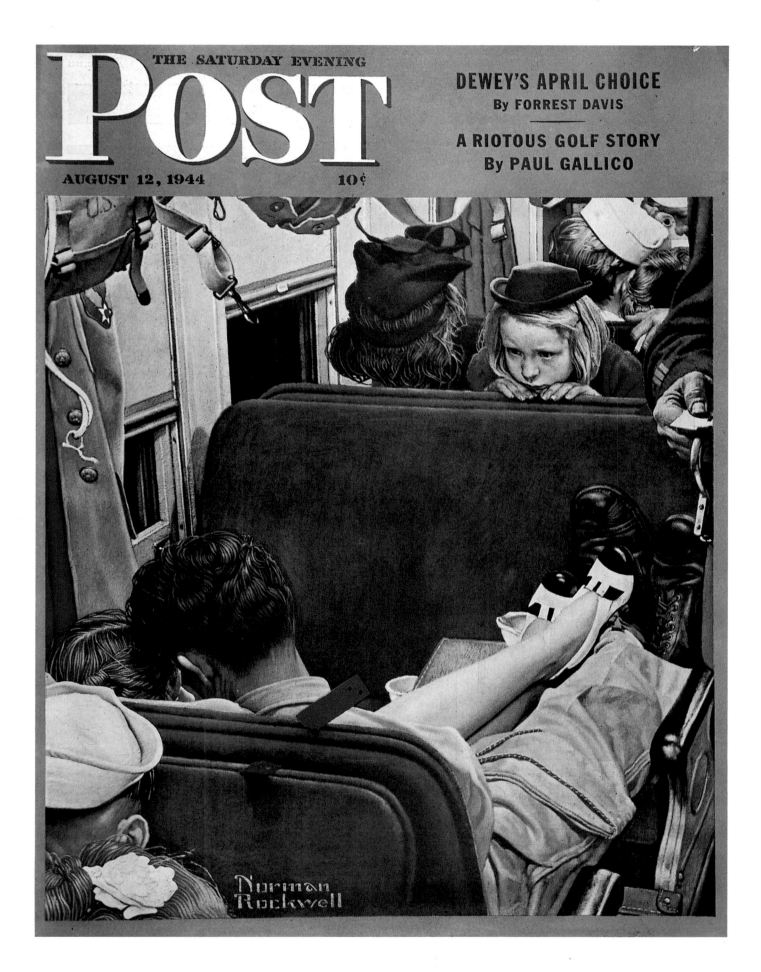

THE SATURDAY EVENING

POST

AUGUST 12, 1944   10¢

DEWEY'S APRIL CHOICE
By FORREST DAVIS

A RIOTOUS GOLF STORY
By PAUL GALLICO

Norman Rockwell

The Voyeur
Post cover, 1944.

The Missed Dance
Post cover, 1937.

THE SATURDAY EVENING POST

An Illustrated Weekly
Founded A°. D°. 1728 by Benj. Franklin

NOTICE TO READER. When you finish reading this copy of The Saturday Evening Post place a U. S. 1-cent stamp on this notice, hand same to any U. S. postal employee, and it will be placed in the hands of our soldiers or sailors at the front. No wrapping, no address. A. S. Burleson, Postmaster General.

JANUARY 26, 1918   5cts. THE COPY

Norman Rockwell

The Wrong Step
Post cover, 1918.

79

THE SATURDAY
EVENING POST

An Illus
Founded A° D

OCTOBER 24, 1936

5c. the Copy

Volume 209, Number 17

THE DEVIL
AND DANIEL WEBSTER—BY STEPHEN VINCENT BENÉT

Left:
The Tantrum
Post cover, 1936.

Above:
Breaking Home Ties
Post cover, 1954.

The Present
Post cover, 1936.

Waiting for the Vet
Post cover, 1952.

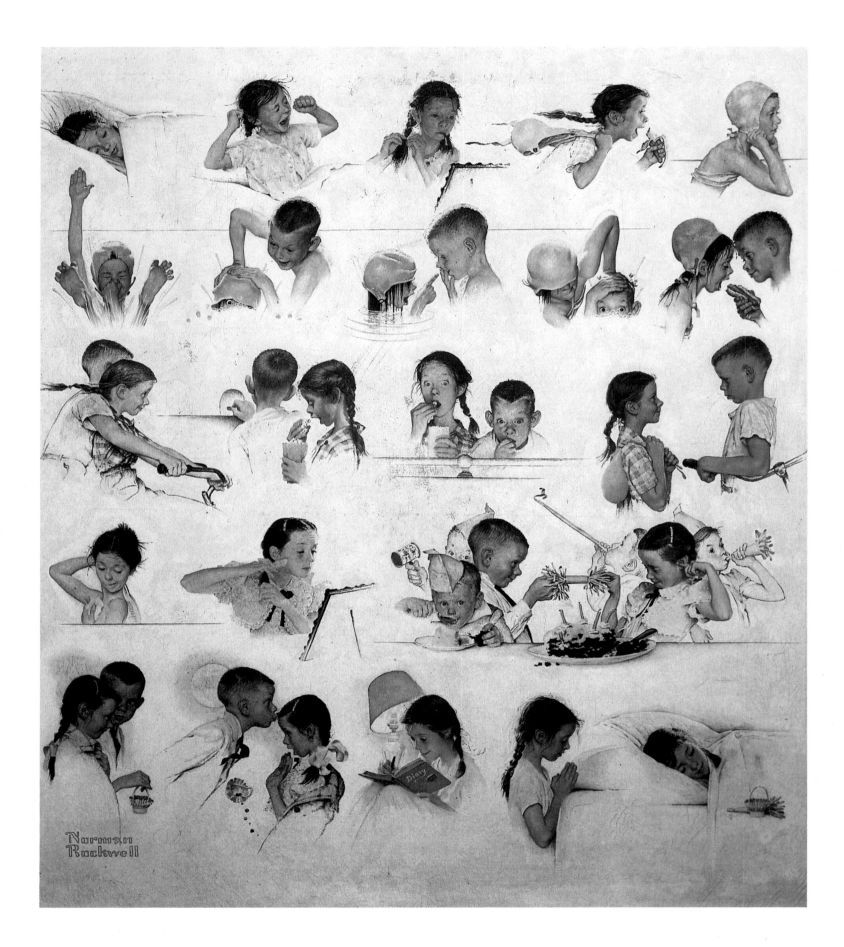

Page 86:
The Spring Tonic
Post cover, 1936.

Page 87:
The Physical
Post cover, 1958.

Norman Rockwell Visits a Country
School
Post illustration, 1946.

Page 92:
Freedom of Speech
Poster, 1943.

Page 93:
Freedom from Fear
Poster, 1943.

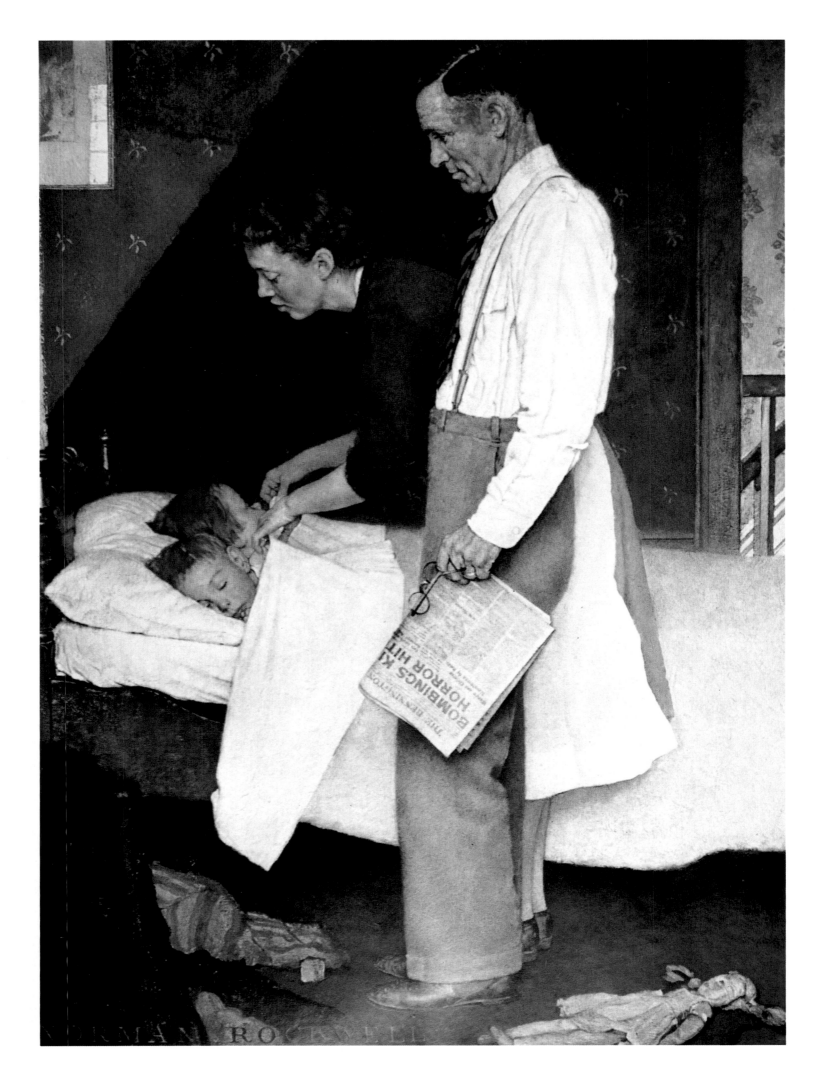

The Peace Corps in Ethiopia
Look illustration, 1966.

Above:
A Family Tree
Post cover, 1959.

Right:
The Fighting Gillises
Post cover, 1944.

Weighing In
Post cover, 1958.

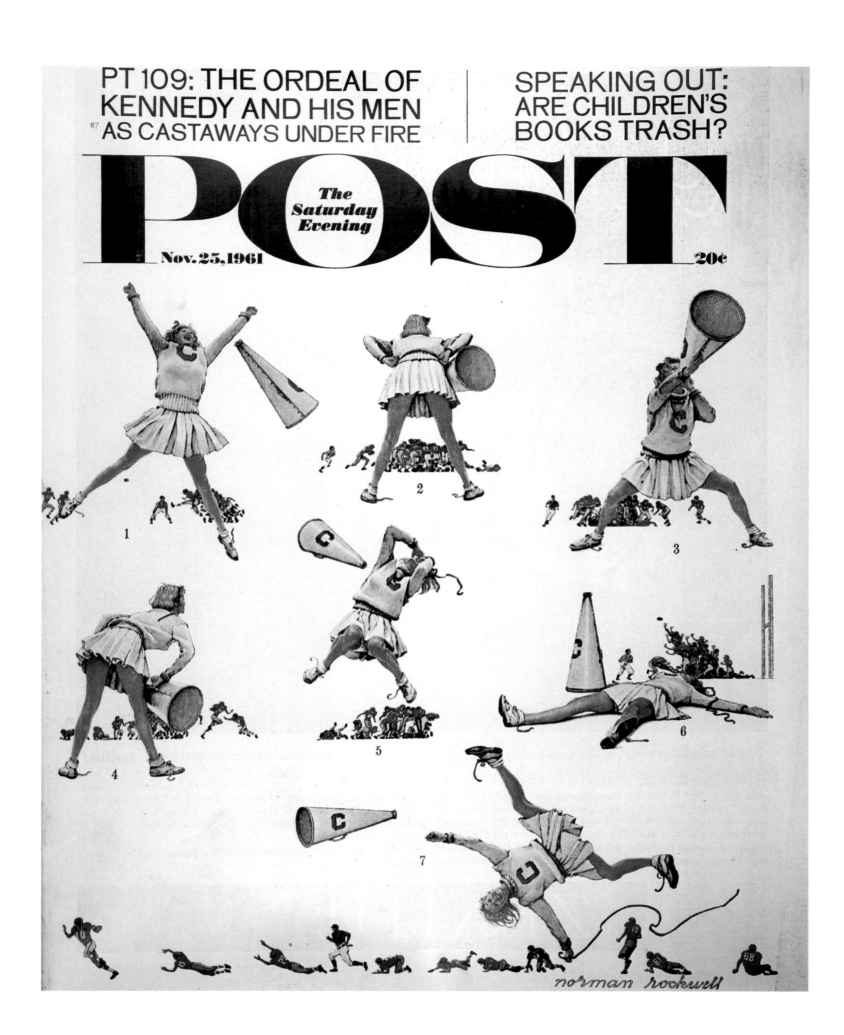

Cheerleader
Post cover, 1961.

Disabled Veteran
Post cover, 1944.

Fixing a Flat
Post cover, 1946.

Elect Casey
Post cover, 1958.

Shuffleton's Barbershop
Post cover, 1950.

Above:
The Marriage License
Post cover, 1955.

Right:
The Partygoers
Post cover, 1935.

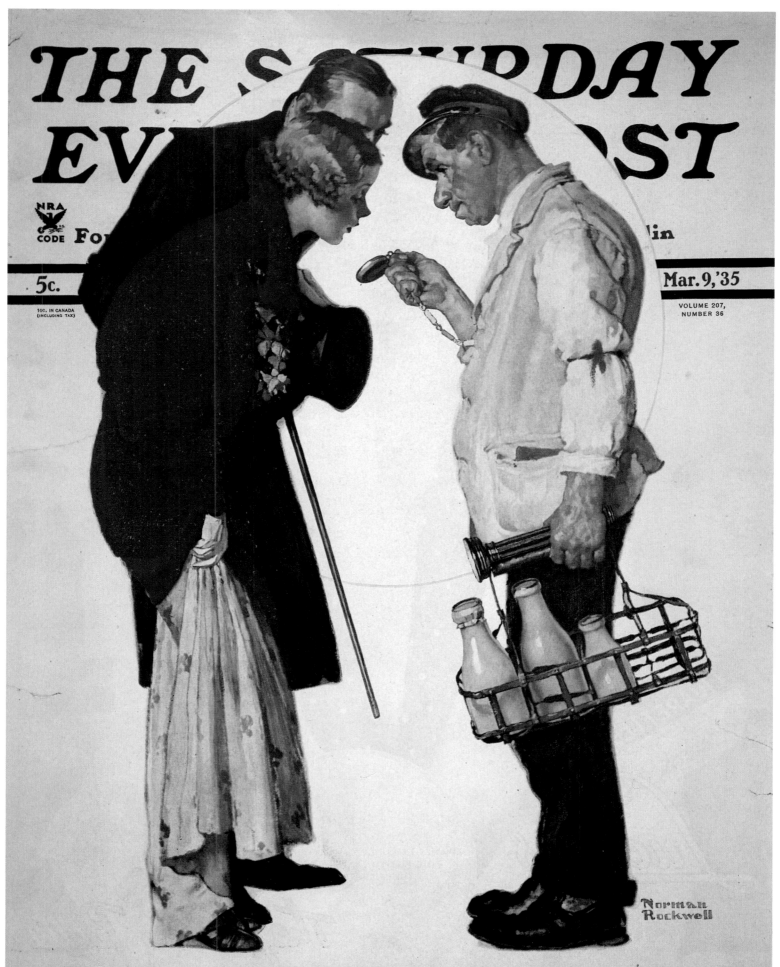

Couple in Rumbleseat
Post cover, 1935.

Willie Gillis in College
Post cover, 1946.

THE SATURDAY EVENING POST
Volume 195, Number 52
JUNE 23, 1923
5c. The Copy 10c. in Canada
Norman Rockwell
George Pattullo—Hugh MacNair Kahler
Sir Philip Gibbs—Will Payne—Sir Basil Thomson
Clarence B. Kelland—Ellis Parker Butler—Norval Richardson

THE SATURDAY EVENING POST

September 2, 1939

5cts.

Left:
Vacation!
Post cover, 1923.

Above:
Marbles Champion
Post cover, 1939.

The Connoiseur
Post cover, 1962.

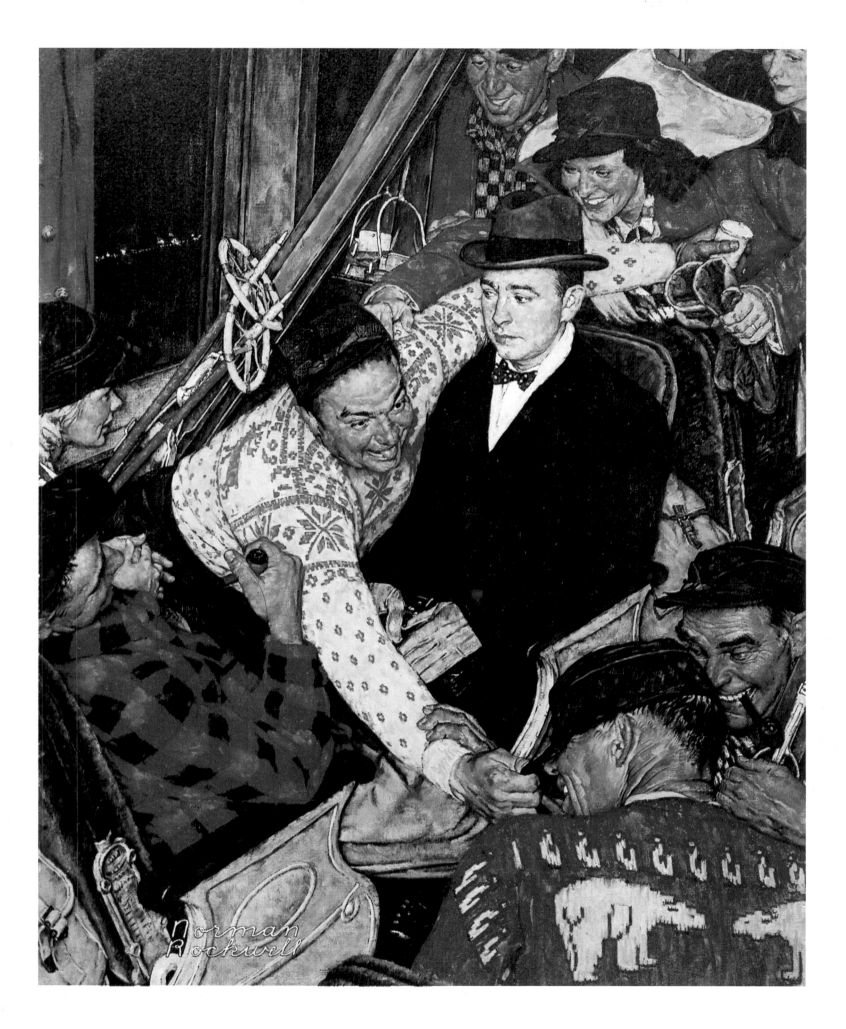

Skiers on a Train
Post cover, 1962.

Thanksgiving
norman rockwell

Left:
The Golden Rule
Post cover, 1961.

Above:
Home for Thanksgiving
Post cover, 1945.

A PILGRIM'S PROGRESS

Left:
Thanksgiving
Post cover, 1943.

Above:
A Pilgrim's Progress
Life cover, 1921.

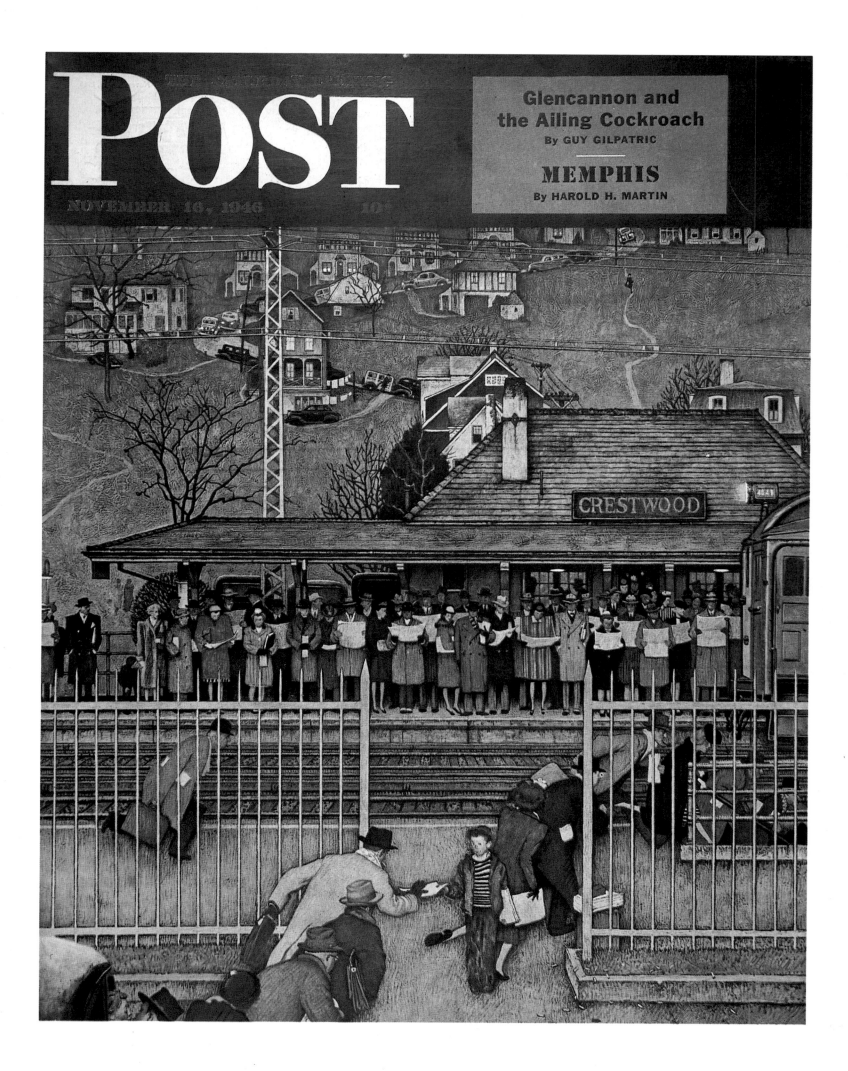

Page 118:
Commuters
Post cover, 1946.

Page 119:
North Western Station, Chicago
Post cover, 1944.

Above:
Dover Coach
Post illustration, 1935

Page 122:
After the Christmas Rush
Post cover, 1947.

Page 123:
Santa on a Subway Train
Post cover, 1940.

THE SATURDAY EVENING POST

Volume 201, Number 33

FEB. 16, '29

Fo...   ...lin

10c. in Canada

5 cts.

Garet Garrett—Mary F. Watkins—I. A. R. Wylie—Horatio Winslow—Kennett Harris
Ben Ames Williams—Clarence Budington Kelland—Rear Admiral T. P. Magruder

Left:
Dreams of Chivalry
Post cover, 1929.

Above:
Homecoming
Post cover, 1948.

125

Astronauts on the Moon
Look illustration, 1967.

Artist Faced with Blank Canvas
Post cover, 1938.

Index of Color Plates